JOURNAL

PETER PAUPER PRESS, INC.
RYE BROOK, NEW YORK

PETER PAUPER PRESS
Fine Books and Gifts Since 1928

OUR COMPANY

In 1928, at the age of twenty-two, Peter Beilenson began printing books on a small press in the basement of his parents' home in Larchmont, New York. Peter—and later, his wife, Edna—sought to create fine books that sold at "prices even a pauper could afford."

Today, still family owned and operated, Peter Pauper Press continues to honor our founders' legacy—and our customers' expectations—of beauty, quality, and value.

—•—

Artwork by Nicola Gregory—Courtesy of Gray Moon Creative Co.

Copyright © 2023
Peter Pauper Press, Inc.
3 International Drive
Rye Brook, NY 10573 USA
All rights reserved
ISBN 978-1-4413-4050-4
Printed in China
7 6 5 4 3 2 1

Visit us at www.peterpauper.com